inside out

children's poets
discuss their work

edited by jonarno lawson

illustrated by jonny hannah

WALKER
BOOKS

Contents

preface

Poems try out poets as much as poets try out poems. As you read through these commentaries you might be surprised by how often an idea, a memory, a word, an image or a rhythm imposed itself on someone, who then was faced with the task of discovering what it meant, or of how to make sense (or nonsense) of it.

Even after a poem has made itself known, it remains puzzling. How does a poem work? No one seems to know, really, but in the commentaries, some very interesting insights into the making of certain poems are offered by those who wrote them.

I hope it's obvious that the selection I made was not in any way exhaustive, or intended to be exclusive – it was hard to limit the selection, but I have not attempted to make anything more (or less) than an enticing sampler of great work in a field that's full of exciting and original voices.

From the beginning I had the idea of approaching this in a way that was "inclusively Anglophile" – as Richard Wilbur put it when he saw the proposed list of poets. While the majority are from England and the United States, there are also poets here from Canada, Australia, Guyana, India, Scotland, New Zealand, Ireland and South Africa. You may notice, as a point of interest, that what rhymes in one accent doesn't necessarily rhyme in another. "Diva" and "beaver", for instance, might rhyme in England, but in North America similarities between the two words remain internal.

I selected poems that surprised me. These poems continue to surprise me. It seems like an embarrassment of riches to have them collected all together in one book. The poets were also asked to explain something about how they came to be. For some reason I expected more overlap in the commentaries, and I was delighted when they came back as varied and fascinating and unalike as the poems they were discussing.

I can't emphasize enough how important it is to read the poems out loud. I don't think you'll be able to appreciate them fully until they've entered your mind through your ears as well as your eyes.

There's so much more I'd like to say about the book, but I'll stop here and let it speak for itself.

JonArno Lawson

OLD WORLD NEW WORLD

Spices and gold once cast a spell
On bearded men in caravels.

New World New World cried history
Old World Old World sighed every tree.

But Indian tribes long long ago
Had sailed this archipelago.

They who were used to flutes of bone
Translated talk of wind on stone.

Yet their feathered tongues were drowned
When Discovery beat its drum.

New World New World – spices and gold
Old World Old World – the legends told.

New World New World – cried history
Old World Old World – sighed every tree.

JOHN AGARD

OLD WORLD NEW WORLD:
COMMENTARY

To mark the beginning of the new century in the
year 2000, there was an anthology of poems I had
great pleasure in editing. It was entitled 'Hello
New' and a number of poets were invited to
contribute a new poem. It was a very open-ended
invitation. The poets were free to go down any road
as long as the word "new" appeared in the poem.
.The results were exciting and intriguing: from
the welcome of a new-born lamb or moving into a new
house to dipping into a new book or having to come
to grips with a new language. The variety of
subject and approach by the poets showed how one
little word can be a springboard into a poem, and
it also gave the reader that thrill of encountering
the word "new" in an unexpected context. That was
the challenge and the fun.
    And that was also the background to the
inspiration for "Old World New World", which first
appeared in that anthology. I was hoping to use
"new" in a not too predictable way. I suppose poets
are always hoping to inject the familiar with
freshness and surprise. As one poet, Ezra Pound,
famously put it: "Poetry is news that stays news."
    So thinking about the word "new" led me to
thinking about "New World", that expression used by
European explorers to describe the Americas and the
islands of the Caribbean, which got their name from
the Carib Indians. These Indians were all part of
a network of Amerindian peoples, including the
Aztecs, Incas and Mayans, who had established
civilizations in the Americas long, long before
Columbus was even born. To these "pre-Columbian"
peoples, whose canoes were sailing the Caribbean

9

many centuries before Columbus' ships, the lands were not exactly new, but to the sixteenth-century Europeans, they were an "undiscovered" world - a New World.

When I was at school in Guyana, where I was born and grew up, there was never any mention that the Vikings and the Phoenicians might also have sailed to the Americas. Our history books always said that the history of the West Indies began with the arrival of Columbus, ignoring the indigenous peoples who had long inhabited the region. In the Guyana rainforest, for example, there are living descendents of ancient Amerindian tribes such as the Carib and the Arawak. You could say their presence is a reminder of old pre-Columbian civilisations. Do they bear witness to an Old World or a New World?

All this, of course, might make interesting history, but interesting history doesn't necessarily make interesting poetry. The poem seeks to invoke the shadow behind the facts and to invite the words not just to relate but to resonate, hopefully in a concise and memorably musical way.

"Old World New World" brings together in one breath a meeting of two worlds, two civilisations, two hemispheres. One of those hemispheres had bows and arrows and no horses. The other had guns and horses. The Amerindian civilisation, as you know, was to be destroyed in what is called the age of conquest or the age of discovery.

But you don't want to overload your poem with too much information, like a room cluttered with furniture. You want to leave space for the reader's imagination to feel at home. Sometimes two rhyming words can bounce off each other like atoms and chime a thought into being. Take "caravels" and "spell". The word "caravels" (light, fast-sailing ships developed by the Portuguese) has a somewhat threatening sound. Columbus and his men arrived in a fleet of "caravels", driven by the desire for gold and exotic spices as if they were under some kind of spell.

For the Amerindian peoples, the so-called New World was rich in ancient myth. For them, the feathers from tropical birds like the macaw and hummingbird were a natural part of their dress as well as something to exchange at the market and on the battlefield. Feathers were also used in medicine and as offerings to the gods. Feathers were companions in rituals and ceremonies.

Why not try reading the poem aloud? Poems get excited when they're read aloud. Yes, try out your "feathered tongues". And I'll keep my fingers crossed that you will no longer be a reader curled up in an armchair, but a wise old shaman or shawoman offering up a few words on the fate of two worlds (Old World New World) and how they will affect each other forever.

FIVE GIRLS

Philomena Cooney
wears green sandals,
yellow ribbons,
silver bangles;
knows three secrets,
lives in a tent
in the middle of a field
near the River Trent.

Arabella Murkhi
speaks in Latin
keeps her cat in,
sleeps in satin.
Went to Turkey
just like that.
Absolutely *loved* it.
Amo amas amat.

Isadora Dooley
loves her jewellery.
Pearls on Sundays,
diamonds Mondays,
rubies Tuesdays,
Wednesdays blue days,
Thursday Friday Saturdays
It-doesn't-really-matter days.

dodgson

Esther Feaver,
opera diva
dressed in beaver,
loved a weaver;
took a breather,
grabbed a cleaver,
now the weaver
will not leave her.

Joan Stone
liked a good moan,
lived on her own
in a mobile home.
The doorbell never rang,
neither did the phone;
so she pressed her ear
to the dialling tone.

CAROL ANN DUFFY

FIVE GIRLS: COMMENTARY

I wrote this poem to amuse my daughter, Ella, when
she was four or five. Two of the names are the
names of real children she knew at the time. One is
a name recalled from my own childhood — Philomena
always sounded strange and exotic to me. I liked
following the rhymes for each name.

My own mother invented similar rhymes to amuse
me when I was a child. The other great influence on
me in childhood was the work of Lewis Carroll.

AQUARIUM

Fishes swim
without a goal
in aquarium or bowl.
We can watch them
through the glass:
bits of sunshine as they pass
in a circle round and round …
Little fish are nowhere bound.
They don't know
the mighty motion
of the waves and
of the ocean.
They must wait
for time to pass
locked up in a cage of glass.

PHILIP DE VOS

AQUARIUM: COMMENTARY

I am a South African writer who started writing
very late in life and since 1984 have published
about twenty-five books, mostly nonsense verse.
In 1996 I was asked by a South African music
organisation to write poems to accompany Saint-
Saëns' "Carnival of the Animals" (1886). A year
after completing a version in Afrikaans, I decided
to write English words. I chose not to translate
the Afrikaans poems directly, but to have each poem
completely new. Here is the Afrikaans poem with
a literal line-by-line translation:

AKWARIUM

Vissies glip	Fishes slip
en vissies gly -	And fishes glide -
'n reënboog	a rainbow
voor my oë verby.	before my eyes.
Vissies swem	Fishes swim
en vissies plas-	and fishes splash -
hoef hul lywe	and never need
nooit te was;	to wash their bodies.
eet nooit boontjies,	They never eat beans
eet nooit kool;	nor cabbage;
gaan ook nimmer	They never need to
na 'n skool.	go to school.
Ek bly hier	I remain here
en hulle dáár	and they remain there
en nooit sal ons	and we will never
kan saambaljaar	romp together.
Vissies swem	Fishes swim
en vissies plas,	and fishes splash
maar tussen ons	but between us
- 'n muur van glas.	- a wall of glass.

After so many years, I cannot remember how the English poem was written. But I did find some scraps of sentences in a notebook, one of many I sometimes grab when I need a clean piece of paper (the same notebook contains notes, addresses and even recipes I jotted down between 1984 and 2006):

Fish all swim without a goal
in the silence of a bowl

You don't know the sea and ocean
You don't feel the mighty motion

divided by a wall of glass

To me the discovery of these jottings shows the truth of A.A. Milne's words: "One of the advantages of being disorderly is that one is constantly making exciting discoveries!" It also proves that the poem was not written in one sitting.

I remember seeing a cartoon of two fish swimming in a goldfish bowl and the baby fish asking the mother: "Are we there yet?" This suggested to me the swimming without an end in sight.

Because Saint-Saëns' piece of music is known as "Aquarium", my phrase "in the silence of a bowl" was later changed to "in aquarium or bowl". I think "a cage of glass" is much better than "a wall of glass", as it emphasizes the idea of being imprisoned.

Looking back, I've also noticed a few things that were intuitively written into the poem, such as the many "s" and "sh" sounds, which suggest the sound of water splashing — swim, glass, bits, sunshine and fishes, watch, sunshine, motion.

But I prefer not to analyse my own poems, and when people read things into my work that I myself did not specifically intend, I start believing that maybe I am cleverer than I thought!

THE STINCHER

When I was three, I told a lie.
To this day that lie is a worry.

Some lies are too big to swallow;
some lies so gigantic they grow

in the dark, ballooning and blossoming;
some lies tell lies and flower,

hyacinths; some develop extra tongues,
purple and thick. This lie went wrong.

I told my parents my brother drowned.
I watched my mother chase my brother's name,

saw her comb the banks with her fingers
down by the river Stincher.

I chucked a stone into the deep brown water,
drowned it in laughter; my father puffing,

found my brother's fishing reel and stool
down by the river Stincher.

I believed in the word disaster.
Lies make things happen, swell, seed, swarm.

Years from that away-from-home lie,
I don't know why I made my brother die.

I shrug my shoulders, when asked, raise my
eyebrows: *I don't know, right, I was three.*

Now I'm thirty-three. That day they rushed me
to the family friends' where my brother sat

undrowned, not frothing at the mouth, sat
innocent, quiet, watching the colourful TV.

Outside, the big mouth of the river Stincher
pursed its lips, sulked and ran away.

JACKIE KAY

THE STINCHER: COMMENTARY

What makes us remember what we remember? What
things, when we look back, stick out in clear
colour? I was interested in guilt and memory in
this poem. We often remember very clearly —
horribly clearly — times in our lives when we have
let ourselves down, or done things we regret or
embarrassed ourselves. This poem is about a lie I
told when I was three. I told my parents that my
brother had drowned in the river. I still don't
know why I did it. But I remember it so vividly
because I felt guilty about it for years.

The images of lies flowering and growing extra
tongues, of lies ballooning and blossoming, are an
attempt to capture the ripple effect of guilt.
Guilt grows in dark closets and multiplies. In
childhood, things loom very large; you can stay
awake worrying about something very small. In
childhood, things quickly get out of proportion.
"Lies make things happen, swell, seed, swarm." I
used the alliteration here so that the reader
continues with that "ssss" sound, snake sound.
There's a contrast in the poem between the
nightmarish, swarming world of the lie, and the
innocent, slightly boring world of the truth. My
brother sits undrowned, not frothing at the mouth,
watching TV. It's all very ordinary. The imagination
is wild! The imagination is a wild beast!

There's also the idea in the poem of the river
enjoying a story being told about itself, as if the
river had encouraged the girl to lie, or had some
part in it. I liked the idea of trying to show how
we can wriggle out of taking responsibility for
what we say; how quickly we turn around and say,
"It wasn't me," or "He made me do it."

The other thing I was trying to capture was the great exhilaration and hysteria involved in telling something totally outlandish. "Drowned it in laughter" – there is a lovely freedom to be found in making things up! Now I write all the time; and in some way writing and lying, making a fiction out of some truths, walking the borderline between truth and fiction, is my bread and butter. I am still walking the banks of the river as a writer.

The Stincher is a river in the south of Scotland near Ballantrae. The incident actually happened by a river near Drymen called The Erskine. But I loved the name Stincher better because it sounded like an onomatopoeic word for lie. I could imagine someone saying, "She told a right Stincher," meaning she told a whopper! In poems you can change the names of rivers and never get accused of lying. That's what I like about writing poems. I can make things up quite legitimately.

IGUANA

Iguana demonstrates the signs
    Of somewhat hasty wrapping:
Beneath its chin a fold of skin
    Hangs downward, loosely flapping.

The quiet victim men forget
    In desert bomb-test sectors;
In Hollywood the pampered pet
    Of horror-film directors

Who need a live iguanadon –
    Oh, then Iguana's happy
To glue a few fake backfins on
    And play its great-grandpappy.

X. J. KENNEDY

IGUANA: COMMENTARY

The little poem "Iguana" came about in what was, for me, an unusual way. A publisher had suggested an alphabetical book of poems for kids, with each poem dealing with a different animal, bird, or insect, arranged from A to Z. I don't usually take on jobs that aren't my own idea, but somehow, the notion was irresistible. Eventually the result was a book called 'Did Adam Name the Vinegarroon?'. The vinegarroon is a kind of scorpion that, when you bother it, gives off the smell of pickles. (Honest, there IS such a creature!)

I started out with Archeopteryx for the letter "A" — that's a long-ago flying lizard, a prehistoric ancestor of our robins and sparrows. But certain letters of the alphabet resisted. They didn't immediately suggest any subjects. Oh oh, I groaned to myself — this job is going to be like pulling teeth. At first the letter "I" seemed one of those hard ones. So I got out my dictionary and began reading through all the words that began with I, looking for animals. There was IBEX, IBIS, but I didn't know what to say about those. Then I came to a picture of an IGUANA, and a lightbulb in my head started flashing. Iguanas, to my surprise, were something I cared about.

And why was that? Back when I was twelve years old, I had been greatly impressed by a movie called "One Million B.C." It wasn't at all historically accurate, for it showed cavemen and dinosaurs living at the same time, but it was a slam-bang rouser of a movie. In one scene, a caveman played by actor Victor Mature waved a spear, holding off a giant iguanadon that was doing its best to gobble up actress Carole Landis, playing a cavewoman with long blonde hair who looked as if she had just stepped out of a beauty shop. Oh boy, I thought, what a thrilling movie. Still, I couldn't help wondering. How in the world had they managed to find a real live dinosaur and bring it to Hollywood?

Then a newspaper story about the movie made it all clear. The film-makers had taken an ordinary iguana, which has spiny projections on its back, and had pasted fins onto them, making the little beast look like its great grand-pappy the iguanadon, that dinosaur of similar name. Then, as it waddled along, the camera zoomed in on it and made it look enormous.

In fact, that iguana wouldn't have been the least bit interested in devouring Carole Landis. It would have preferred a nice juicy fly.

Later on, another news report had struck me, haunted me, stayed in my memory. When atomic bomb tests were conducted in New Mexico, some lizards had been blown up along with the bomb. Had they been some poor, innocent iguanas who happened to live on the test site? I didn't know for sure, but reckoned they might have been.

All of that miscellaneous information was material for a poem. I started scribbling lines. It has been so many years since then that to tell you the truth I don't remember much about the actual writing of the poem. It probably had to be worked over and revised a few times. Most poems do, even if at first they quickly emerge in rough form. I wish I could get things right the first time, but that practically never happens, so I just keep writing and writing and trying to get a poem right, and filling up my wastebasket.

THE OCTOPUS AND THE SEAHORSE

The seahorse bowed to the octopus
and asked if she would please
join him in his night-time dance
around the coral keys.
Her shyness put his aquatic
quasi-equestrian heart at ease.
She blinked her eyes and then she bowed,
bending her many knees.

They danced, they danced –
the Octopus-Seahorse dance –
in their many-legged
multi-coloured barnacle-covered pants.
They danced, they danced –
and their twirling was much enhanced
by the current above the seabed floor
and their oceanic trance.

JONARNO LAWSON

26

THE OCTOPUS AND THE
SEAHORSE: COMMENTARY

Few poets know why they've written a poem until
after they've written it, and even then it isn't
always clear. But usually it's possible to figure
out where certain ideas and images in the poem come
from.

HOW FEELINGS SOMETIMES TURN INTO ANIMALS

The octopus and the seahorse are both shy,
gentle sea animals. They are also hard to
categorize — what is an octopus exactly? And what
is a seahorse? Is it a fish? I often find it hard
to say who or what I am as well. I'm also shy, and
like to think I'm gentle. In other words it's very
possible that I thought of the octopus and the
seahorse because they reminded me of myself in some
way.

HOOFBEATS FIRST

Very often, the rhythm of a poem comes before
the poem itself. I sometimes find myself tapping
with my fingers before I think of a single word I'm
going to write. It's a bit like hearing hoofbeats
before you can see the horse or the rider.

THE MYSTERIOUS MIGRATIONS OF MEMORIES

When I was eight years old, I moved briefly to
Miami, Florida. Though I spent only a few months
there over thirty years ago, I remember it as if it
were yesterday. I have clear memories of the
surprising sea creatures I watched from the shore,
or found washed up on the beach. Many of these
creatures, over the years, have crept out of my
memories and into my poems.

A STRIKING IMAGE

The seahorse is very small; the octopus is,
comparatively, very large; this creates a comic

element to their attraction. It also makes for a
striking image (I think so, anyway). At the same
time, it's touching that they're not concerned
about their obvious difference in size, and that
they're being so formal with, and considerate to,
each other.

IF THE POEM HAS MOVEMENT AND STRIKING IMAGES, IT
WILL, WITH A BIT OF IMAGINATION, RUN LIKE A SHORT
MOVIE IN YOUR MIND.

In this poem there is constant movement. The two
creatures are very formal and almost cautious at
the beginning, but by the end they've let
themselves go completely. When I think of this poem
it runs through my mind like a small movie: the
seahorse bows, the octopus blinks, they begin their
dance – a whirling dance – and, as they whirl about
the coral, even the current adds something to their
dancing. Either from the whirling or from
happiness, or from both, they go into a trance, and
this adds something to the dance too – they're not
self-conscious anymore. Their movements have become
free.

ARE THOUGHTS THE PLAYTHINGS OF WORDS OR WORDS
THE PLAYTHINGS OF THOUGHTS?

As far as the writing of the poem goes, I was
proudest of the ridiculous phrase "aquatic quasi-
equestrian". It was the hardest, and at the same
time the most fun part of the poem to write. The
"kw" sound is not a common one in English, and to
find three "kw" words that would run together
naturally while still making sense (and at the same
time sounding like comical nonsense) wasn't easy.

When I first wrote the poem, I had it nearly all
done on the first go, aside from those difficult
fifth and sixth lines ("Her shyness put his
aquatic/quasi-equestrian heart at ease"); I had no
idea what to put there. I left it blank. Then,

after a few weeks, I put in "Her hesitating shyness put his equestrian heart at ease" – I was on the right track when I came up with the word "equestrian", which means "relating to horse-riding", but the line was dull. So I kept thinking about it, on and off, and finally it occurred to me that "aquatic" would work well. And then, as I was trying to figure out a new line with "aquatic", the word "quasi" popped into my head, and I had it.

I couldn't believe my luck: I knew what "quasi" meant, but I couldn't suppress a superstitious impulse to double-check it in the dictionary.

Once I start looking at a poem from many different angles, dozens of different associations crop up, and it's difficult to know which were relevant to the making of the poem, and which are associations or memories triggered or unearthed by the poem after it was made. Trying to figure out how a poem works (or doesn't) is every bit as entertaining as writing it, I think. It's just as easy to slip into the realm of nonsense, and, simultaneously, to make unexpected discoveries.

ALLIGATOR PIE

Alligator pie, alligator pie,
If I don't get some I think I'm gonna die.
Give away the green grass, give away the sky,
But don't give away my alligator pie.

Alligator stew, alligator stew,
If I don't get some I don't know what I'll do.
Give away my furry hat, give away my shoe,
But don't give away my alligator stew.

Alligator soup, alligator soup,
If I don't get some I think I'm gonna droop.
Give away my hockey-stick, give away my hoop,
But don't give away my alligator soup.

DENNIS LEE

SOMETHING-OR-OTHER

STORE

ALLIGATOR PIE: COMMENTARY

One day I didn't go to the store, and I came back with alligator pie. And then I went to the store.

It's true. It was 1966, and I had two young daughters. And since my wife and I loved Mother Goose, we were reading lots of nursery rhymes at bedtime. After a while I started making up rhymes of my own. The old rhymes are wonderful, I thought, but why not have some new ones too?

On this particular day, I had to go buy something or other at the store. I got on my bike, and I headed off down our street in central Toronto. But after about twenty seconds, something interrupted me.

My legs were going around and around as I pedalled, and there was a particular rhythm when my left foot, and then my right, pressed the pedal down. I began to hear snatches of words that echoed the rhythm: *All-i-ga-tor pie* ... *All-i-ga-tor pie* ... Da *dum*-da, da *dum*-da ... I *think* I'm gonna *cry* (*sigh? die?*) ...

I had no idea where this had come from. The words were ridiculous, and I wished they'd go away; I had to buy the something-or-other, after all, and I wanted to get home and get back to my writing. But more of these nutty words were arriving: *Give* away the (*dump*-itty-dum) ... *Give* away the (*fly? sky? eye?*) ... But *don't* give a-way my ... alligator *pie*.

The wretched thing wouldn't stop – now I was hearing alligator stew too. Eventually I couldn't keep all the words in my head. So in exasperation I turned the bike around, rode back home, and scribbled down as much as I could remember: a couple of verses, with lots of holes. Thank goodness I got rid of that, I thought. Then I rode

to the store, bought the something-or-other, and
that was the end of that.

Except there was a little more. I finished the
poem later on, and I read it to my daughters and
other kids, and it turned out that whenever a child
heard it, she couldn't forget it. So it went into
my first children's book, and in fact it became the
title poem. And now there are kids all around the
world who chant that rhyme, and most of them have
never heard of Dennis Lee.

Which is fine by me. I'm just glad I didn't keep
going to buy the something-or-other.

THE MAN FROM THE LAND OF FANDANGO

The man from the land of Fandango
Is coming to pay you a call,
With his tricolour jacket and polka-dot tie
And his calico trousers as blue as the sky
And a hat with a tassel and all.
And he bingles and bangles and bounces,
He's a bird! He's a bell! He's a ball!
The man from the land of Fandango
Is coming to pay you a call.
Oh, whenever they dance in Fandango
The bears and the bison join in,
And the baboons with bassoons make a musical sound,
And the kangaroos come with a hop and a bound,
And the dinosaurs join in the din.
And they tingle and tongle and tangle
Till tomorrow turns into today.
Then they stop for a break and a drink and a cake
In their friendly fandandical way.

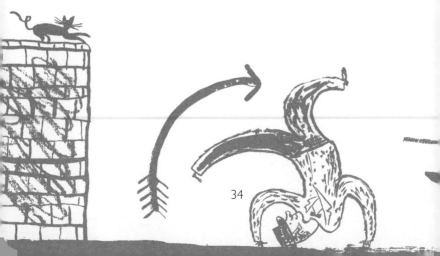

The man from the land of Fandango
Is given to dancing and dreams.
He comes in at the door like a somersault star
And he juggles with junkets and jam in a jar
And custards and caramel creams.
And he jingles and jongles and jangles
As he dances on ceilings and walls,
And he appears every five hundred years
So you'd better be home when he calls.

MARGARET MAHY

THE MAN FROM THE LAND OF FANDANGO: COMMENTARY

Sometimes it is hard for a poet to say exactly
where poems come from. Poems sometimes tell stories
or they pass some wonderful picture into your mind
— something beautiful, something funny. A lot of
the poems that I manage to write are to do with the
sound of words. When I read them afterwards,
I think, "There are jokes with the sound of words
hidden in these lines". I write the poems down on
a page, but I like to think that some reader
somewhere will actually say the poem aloud. It
would mean that the poem is set free from the page
and will be heard out in the open air.

There are many moments of amazement in life. On
an ordinary day we may see something that takes us
by surprise; something as simple as a spring
flower, or a cat creeping along the top of a wall.
This morning I saw four birds flying across the sky
in a certain formation — I couldn't tell if they
were ducks or wild geese. I was filled with an
unexpected astonishment. I forgot all the things
I was supposed to be doing and stood staring up at
them. And of course there are other astonishing
moments when something really remarkable is taking
place, when some wonderful gymnast is turning
somersaults and cartwheels, or a clown suddenly
appears in a supermarket and juggles balls, making
jokes as he (or she) juggles. "The Man from the
Land of Fandango" is about a moment like that. Of
course, the poem is partly a joke about
astonishment, but I think it might also have
something mysterious about it hidden in the words.
And I like to think that, as you read the poem or
say the poem or hear the poem, colourful pictures

will fill your head. You will actually see the Man from Fandango juggling custards and caramel creams.

Writing this poem I imagined people living an ordinary life, but then, suddenly, everything changes around them. The Man from the Land of Fandango – from the land of the imagination – leaps into the room like a somersault star. Everyone can see him as he twists and turns and juggles.

Of course, moments of astonishment come much more frequently than every five hundred years. That is a joke in the poem. In real life, astonishment and wonder can leap in on you at any moment. You do need to be at home in your own head when they call, however. Once I had the idea for this poem, once I had the image of that bounding man of Fandango in my head, I don't think it took me long to write it. It just seemed to bounce along out of the end of my pen.

When I had it written down on paper, I began to make changes. I liked the idea of using words beginning with the same letter because I thought alliteration would make the words a little bit tongue-twister-ish, fun to say aloud or to hear secretly in your head as you read the poem: "He bingles and bangles and bounces/He's a bird! He's a bell! He's a ball!" As I write poems down I always read them aloud to myself just to see how they sound in the outside air.

RIDING WEST FROM LITTLE BEAR

I ride a horse called Secrets
A lively dapple-grey
His hoofbeats echo down the trail
They call the Milky Way

Past a stampede of meteors
Down the ravines of space
And over the deserts of silver dust
Watchfully we pace

We journey on with hopeful hearts
Though the way's long and far
But sometimes halt and light a fire
Upon some lonesome star.

ADRIAN MITCHELL

RIDING WEST FROM LITTLE BEAR: COMMENTARY

When I was a child I was given two globes. One was
the wonderful usual kind, with all the countries of
the world trying to squash into the seven
continents, many of them coloured pinkish-red to
indicate they were supposed to belong to the King
of England. But the other globe was very dark and
blue all over, sprinkled with white circles and
dots which represented the planets and stars and
galaxies. And there was our planet Earth, in the
middle of the Milky Way. And I was out there too,
with my mother and father and my brother Jimmy and
my two globes. By day I lived on the Earth globe,
but by night I dreamed on the dark blue Sky globe.
So space has always seemed like home to me. I love
the sun and stars and planets and meteors and
especially our gentle moon.

For most of my life I have been half in love
with America. It started with American jazz, which
was my rebel music when I was a teenager. I was
excited by American comics and then by American
poets like Walt Whitman and Theodore Roethke and
Kenneth Patchen and Allen Ginsberg. Most of the
movies I saw were American.

I never saw the USA until I was 22, and then I
took a train ride right across it, from New York to
Seattle. I was enchanted by the incredible variety
of landscapes and climates – and by the
friendliness of the people. I've been back many
times, though nowadays my feelings about the USA
are very mixed, because of the stupid and cruel
wars conducted by the American government.

But even before I heard jazz, my brother and I
were given cowboy suits. Our cowboy trousers had

sheepskin chaps down the front of the legs. My
brother's chaps were white, like everyone else's.
But mine were black wool. At first I was unhappy
about this, but somehow my lovely mother persuaded
me that they were very stylish.

That was a thousand years ago, but still I
sometimes play cowboy in my daydreams. I jump off a
train in a strange city and mutter under my breath,
"I've come to clean up this town." But I've really
only come to perform my poems.

As a child I used to ride an enormous German ex-
cavalry horse called Baroness. One day she stopped
suddenly on a steep hill, but I kept going over her
head and woke up in bed. It stopped me riding, but
I still admire horses.

"Riding West from Little Bear" started as a poem
about riding over a desert. I climbed on the horse
and decided that he was called "Secrets" – which is
one of my favourite words. It's a word like a
parcel that I want to unwrap and find what's in it.
"Dapple-grey" is another special word for me, for
the sound of it and its rhyme with Apple Day.

I was riding across a rocky landscape towards
a ramshackle western town called Little Bear. But
then I realized that it wasn't a town I was headed
for, it was the Little Bear itself, the famous
star, child of the Great Bear. So we must be riding
through space. But I hung on to Western words like
"trail" and "stampede", "ravines" and "lonesome".
Then I saw that the trail underneath the hooves of
Secrets was the Milky Way itself. And then I saw
the meteors stampeding and said: Slow down,
Secrets. I want to take it all in. It was beautiful
out there in space, I felt free and easy. But I
kept watch just in case of any trouble.

The poem doesn't have an end. It just pauses, on
some lonesome star. I light a fire to cook a meal

and warm us overnight. I feed and water Secrets. I say to him: "You know what? I don't mind if this journey goes on for ever."

What's the point of going on? To find some kind of peace. Maybe when we reach the Little Bear.

Adrian Mitchell asks that none of his poems be used in exams or tests.

DIDGERIDOO

Catfish
take catnaps on seabeds
Sticklebacks
stick like glue
Terrapins
are terrific with needles
But what does a didgery do?

Bloodhounds
play good rounds of poker
Chihuahuas
do nothing but chew
Poodles
make puddles to paddle in
But what does a didgery do?

A puffin
will stuff in a muffin
A canary
can nearly canoe
Hummingbirds
hum something rotten
But what does a didgery do?

Tapeworms
play tapes while out jogging
Flies
feed for free at the zoo
Headlice
use headlights at night-time
But what does a didgery do?

What does a didgery
What does a didgery
What does a didgery do?

ROGER McGOUGH

DIDGERIDOO: COMMENTARY

A didgeridoo is a musical instrument made from
eucalyptus wood or bamboo pipe, invented by native
Australians which not only makes a lovely dark
sound but has a fine name.

Kedgeree is a popular breakfast dish of lightly
curried rice, smoked fish and hard-boiled eggs,
originating from India. The poem started life as
a joke I scribbled in one of the little notebooks
I always carry with me:

> What is fishy, eggy
> and plays music
> at breakfast ?
>
> A Kedgeree doo

I had obviously been thinking about the word
didgeridoo, because next to that scribble I had
written:

> But what does a didgery
> Do.

And having asked myself that question, I had to
answer it. But not right away.

Several weeks later, in another notebook,
a larger one that I keep on my desk, I sat down to
answer the question, and the poem took wing once
I imagined the didgery as an animal.

The next step was to assemble a list of other creatures whose names I could play with.

"Terrapins" for instance suggested "pins and needles" and "terrific" uses the first four letters of "terrapin" too. Sticklebacks sticking, chihuahuas chewing, hummingbirds humming; I bet you could make up a completely different list to create your own version of the poem.

From the outset, I realised that I needed to find words to rhyme with "do" and this wasn't difficult, but a more interesting challenge was to find unusual "internal" rhymes that would amuse the reader and keep the poem on its toes: "Bloodhounds /good rounds", "Puffin/stuffin/muffin", "Canary/can nearly", "Headlice/headlights".

My proudest moment was when Rolf Harris, no mean didgeridoo player himself, performed the poem on children's television.

THE WISHING BONE

It happened on a winter's day
(The air was cold, the sky was grey):
Out walking in the woods alone,
I came upon a wishing bone.

I picked it up and wished the sky
As warm and gentle as July.
I wished sweet music in the air
And flowers growing everywhere.

I wished an apple orchard and
A beach with sugar-flavoured sand,
A lake, a little birch canoe.
And everything I wished came true.

I wished down tinier than a flea,
Wished up above the tallest tree,
I wished me as a wolf, a shark,
A firefly shining in the dark,

A blade of grass, an ocean wave,
A bear asleep inside its cave.
I wished a talking daffodil.
I wished a dragon I could kill.

I wished a flock of purple geese.
I wished the world eternal peace.
I wished a pair of angel's wings.
And then a thousand other things.

But after many days had past,
Each wish seemed easier than the last,
And I felt bored as stiff as stone,
And wished the wishing off the bone.

And suddenly I stood at ease
Among the bare and patient trees
One ordinary winter's day.
The air was cold. The sky was grey.

STEPHEN MITCHELL

THE WISHING BONE: COMMENTARY

All of a sudden, out of nowhere, I came upon the phrase *I came upon a wishing bone*. Though it was the poem's fourth line, it was the first one I heard in my inner ear. I knew it was the beginning of a small adventure.

I was sitting at my desk in a garage in Berkeley, California. It was winter, and the garage was impossible to heat, so I would wear a down coat, stick my legs into a sleeping bag, slip on a pair of fingerless gloves, and settle down to work.

I was as intrigued to discover my line as the narrator of the poem must have been to make *his* discovery. Actually, the whole poem was contained in that one line. I knew that it would be about finding and getting beyond magic. It would also be about the four-beat iambic couplet, one of the simplest verse forms in the English language. The challenge would be how to vary the rhythms from stanza to stanza so that they would always be slightly different and always seem fresh.

The first three lines wrote themselves quickly. It *was* a winter's day; the air *was* cold. After *alone* conveniently appeared, to rhyme with *bone*, I thought, *Hmm. Where is it going to go from here?*

Well, of course, summer: that was easy enough. The child who was the speaker of the poem (I imagined him as being six years old) started with three obvious wishes: not only summer and flowers, but *sweet music* (the phrase had an Elizabethan feeling to it). Then he wished an apple orchard, which I hadn't expected. But the bigger surprise was that the line rhymed on *and*. That was interesting; up to this point the rhymes had been fairly conventional.

I liked it that there was a surprise in every line.

Sugar-flavoured sand, for example. The wishes
expanded as my little narrator began to test the
limits of wishes. And the poem was still just twelve
lines old.

The challenge here was to suggest a whole universe
of wish-fulfilment within a few stanzas. The narrator
turned out to be a junior Walt Whitman: he becomes
everything he can think of, from the vast to the
tiny, from the dangerous to the heroic. I
particularly liked the line *I wished the world eternal peace.*
This comes close to the essence of what most people
think of as prayer, and though it's a compassionate
desire, there's a hugely egotistic thought behind it:
If I were God, I could do a better job with the world.

How would the poem conclude? I knew that the
narrator would have to see that "My will be done" is
a dead end, that ultimately happiness can come only
from the deep acceptance of reality expressed in "Thy
will be done." How could I convey that in a couple of
stanzas?

It all unfolded naturally in the wake of the word
"But". I liked the expression *I felt bored as stiff as stone,*
because it brought to life the cliché "bored stiff".
The next line startled me a bit. There was a brave
finality to the boy's decision, with no chance for
second thoughts. What is the world like when you've
let go of control — of whatever control you thought
you had? You get to live in a truth that even the
dearest wish can't hold a candle to.

The last stanza has a Zen simplicity to it. The key
words are *at ease.* When what you want is what you have,
of course you're at ease. What is special about this
state of ease is the "nothing special" of it. And I
particularly liked that these lines grouped themselves
three by one, rather than two by two. That delighted
my ear as much as the meaning delighted my mind.

COLOURS CRACKLE, COLOURS ROAR

Red shouts a loud, balloon-round sound.
  Black crackles like noisy grackles.
  Café clickety-clicks its wooden sticks.
  Yellow sparks and sizzles, tzz-tzz.
White sings, *Ay*, her high, light note.
Verde rustles leaf-secrets, swish, swish.
Gris whis-whis-whispers its kitten whiskers.
    Silver ting-ting-a-ling jingles.
    Azul coo-coo-coos like *pajaritos* do.
Purple thunders and rum-rum-rumbles.
    Oro blares, a brassy, brass tuba.
Orange growls its striped, rolled roar.
      Colours Crackle, Colours Roar.

azul (ah-ZUHL) : blue
café (kah-FEH) : brown
gris (GREECE) : grey
oro (OH-roh) : gold
pajaritos (pah-hah-REE-toce) : little birds
verde (VER-deh) : green

PAT MORA

50

COLOURS CRACKLE, COLOURS ROAR: COMMENTARY

I love colours, especially bright ones. I grew up
in a bilingual home in El Paso, Texas, right on the
U.S./Mexico border. Among my favorite memories are
visits with my family to the market in Juarez, the
Mexican city across the Rio Grande. At the market,
we'd hear Spanish and music in the air, we'd smell
fresh fruits and warm tortillas, and we'd see
colours everywhere — tomatoes, toys, pinatas.
  Years later, when I was living in Cincinnati,
Ohio, I was at a children's book conference and
a teacher or librarian said, "You write poetry for
adults. Why don't you write a poetry collection for
children?" Hmm, I thought. Good idea. Far away from
the Southwest desert I usually write about, among
maples and oaks, I began to play with a poem about
colours, since they delight me. We usually think
about how colours look, how we experience them with
our eyes. But how do colours sound, I asked myself.
Now that seemed like a good writing journey to
make. I began to mull, to noodle around a bit with
colours and words, asking myself: How does red
sound? How does black sound? How does orange sound?
I sometimes doodle while I noodle, so when I asked
the question about red, I drew a balloon. I liked
the idea of red sounding like a balloon, but I also
wanted the sounds in that line to sound round, so I
played until I had a line I liked: "Red shouts a
loud, balloon-round sound."

I like to have students say the lines of this
poem after me, so that our mouths shape the colour
sounds. How does black sound, I asked myself?
(Writers are always talking or muttering to
themselves.) When I visit South Texas, I like to

hear the cries of shiny black birds called
grackles. People think they're pests, but I like
their noise, and I like the sound of the word
grackle. Say it out loud. Fun, isn't it? And as
soon as we say it, we want to pair the word with
crackle, yes? "Black crackles like noisy grackles."

Because I'm lucky enough to speak both English
and Spanish and have the opportunity to play with
words and sounds in both languages, I wanted to
include some Spanish as I usually do.

The third line of the poem, "*Café* clickety-clicks
its wooden sticks", has many hard "k" sounds. Using
the word brown wouldn't have worked at all, and
since sticks are brown, the Spanish word with its
hard "k" sound, seemed a good choice.

I enjoyed thinking of colour after colour and
what sound it might make. Then I'd decide whether
to use English or Spanish words or both. "*Azul* coo-
coo-coos like *pajaritos* do". *Azul* means blue. The word
"blue" works musically with "coo-coo-coo", but the
"oo" sound in *azul* stays in the air longer. Also,
the word *pajaritos* (*pah har EE tohs*), birds, has four
syllables and a sweet sound that stretches that
line in the poem.

Colour by colour I listened, which is what poets
do, isn't it? We're listening to the ideas, even
the wacky ideas that come to us, and we're
listening to the words themselves, sometimes in
more than one language. We're listening to how the
words sound side-by-side, and in the line.
I enjoyed listening to yellow, white, *verde*, *gris*,
silver, purple, and *oro*.

It was great fun to end with the sound of the
colour orange. I wanted a big sound to end the poem
since it began with red's "loud, balloon-round
sound". Orange, the fruit, was not going to make
much of a racket, was it? But what if the colour

orange roared or growled? And what if that growl
were striped like a -----? "Orange growls its
striped, rolled roar." Students always know what
orange-coloured animal is making that "ROAR".

I hope that you will write your own poem about
how colours sound to you. And share it too.

SUN IS LAUGHING

This morning she got up
On the happy side of the bed,
Pulled back
The grey sky-curtains
And poked her head
Through the blue window
Of heaven,
Her yellow laughter
Spilling over,
Falling broad across the grass,
Brightening the washing line,
Giving more shine
To the back of a ladybug
And buttering up all the world.

Then, without any warning,
As if she was suddenly bored,
Or just got sulky
Because she could hear no one
Giving praise
To her shining ways,
Sun slammed the sky-window closed,
Plunging the whole world
Into greyness once more.

O Sun, moody one,
How can we live
Without the holiday of your face?

GRACE NICHOLS

54

SUN IS LAUGHING: COMMENTARY

The changeability of the English weather always
keeps me on my toes, and in a way was the
inspiration for the poem. Since living in England
(for the past thirty years) I've developed much
more of a "weather-eye". In Guyana, where I grew
up, we take the sun for granted. No one says, "What
a glorious day." We only tend to comment on the
weather when it's raining.

Living in England has changed all that. I am
much more aware of what's happening outside, and
the weather is a hot topic of conversation in our
home, whether we're moaning, with an exaggerated
shiver, at someone who's left the front door open
in winter or using the sun as an excuse to go
out: "It's going to be wet and cold tomorrow. Better
make the most of it."

On a nice sunny day it's difficult to get me to
stay at home. It was one such day that triggered
the poem. I was in high spirits as I could see the
sun beckoning me to come and bathe in its glow.
I got dressed quickly — I knew things can change
rapidly. But by the time I was ready, much to my
disappointment, it was dark and grey again. It was
as if someone had switched off a light in the sky
or closed a window, blotting out the sun.

So at one level you could say that "Sun Is
Laughing" is about the feel-good effect that the
sun has on me. At a wider level, it's a slightly
playful homage. Even though the different English
seasons have their own magic (I love the colours of
autumn) I still miss the amazing yellowness of the
sunlight back in the Caribbean.

The poem was written fairly quickly. It came at
one sitting. I have to work much more at some of my

other poems. I think the reason for this is that the sun has always figured strongly in my imagination and I'd been collecting my impressions for a long time, without consciously thinking about it. That morning, the sight of the sun suddenly going in disappointed my "weather-eye" but triggered the joy of a poem. I saw sun as a temperamental teenage girl going off in a huff to her room (my apologies to teenage girls, but I do have two daughters of my own).

I hardly made any changes to the poem once I'd written it. In the beginning I thought of Sun getting up on the "right side of bed" as a sign that she was in a good mood. We speak of someone getting out of the "wrong side of bed" when they wake up in a bad mood. In the end, I chose "happy side of the bed". Happy seemed right.

I like reading this particular poem. The way it unfolds down the page in a simple narrative, telling a little story. I particularly like the ending –   O Sun, moody one,
                  How can we live
                  without the holiday of your face?
because I hadn't thought of the line "the holiday of your face" until I had actually written it. Interestingly, the word "holiday" comes from the words "holy day."

In the act of writing a poem, ideas and feelings and images link up in surprising ways. You might ask why I made the sun female when the moon is usually seen as female. Well, in many cultures, including in some of our own Amerindian folk stories, the sun is seen as a goddess figure with a glittering mirror and this is what might have prompted me to make Sun in the poem a young woman.

SUPPLE CORD

My brother, in his small white bed,
held one end.
I tugged the other
to signal I was still awake.
We could have spoken,
could have sung
to one another.
We were in the same room
for five years,
but the soft cord
with its little frayed ends
connected us
in the dark,
gave comfort
even if we had been bickering
all day.
When he fell asleep first
and his end of the cord
dropped to the floor,
I missed him terribly,
though I could hear his even breath
and we had such long and separate lives
ahead.

NAOMI SHIHAB NYE

SUPPLE CORD: COMMENTARY

A few years ago, I was spending the night in an old
inn in Michigan, when I found myself staring at
a satiny, braided white cord with fringes, holding
back the curtain. Ping! Another similar cord
I hadn't thought of for many years popped back into
my brain.

The first cord used to function as a "telephone
line" between my brother's bed and mine, in our
childhood home in St Louis. I don't know where we
got it. We didn't "talk" on it - we just tugged it
back and forth. Different cord, different state,
whole different era, but - something felt connected
again. An image linked to another image. At that
moment, I really missed my brother.

I love the way connections can click together
and link up unexpectedly. Something you did not
realize was still living in the deep well of your
brain rises to the surface and shines again.

THE SHAPE

Since the poem was about a cord, it needed to be
long and skinny.

Writing a poem is always an experiment.

Which words do you choose, what shape do the
lines take? The more you write, the more you feel
mysterious little instincts humming inside the
words. I like a poem that takes you into the scene
right away. I hope a reader can easily "see" the
cord stretching between the brother and sister in
the two twin beds on either side of the room.

Rituals between people who know each other well
can be comforting. I wanted the poem to suggest
that we held onto the cord's two ends many nights
in our early lives, and we liked it. It was our
quiet little tradition. When my mother read this

poem, about 45 years later, she said, "What cord?"

When I was about 11, our parents turned the garage into another bedroom and moved me out there. I hated it. Not only was I scared of the mice and bugs who might find me in the place the washing machine and car used to live, there was no cord long enough to reach my brother on the other side of the house. This information is not in the poem. But I thought of it while writing. I have always been interested in what we do not include when we write a poem. Every written poem has another silent, unspoken world around it.

MEMORY RISING

I had not thought of the fact my brother always fell asleep first for many years. But when I saw the cord in Michigan, that memory rose too. I'd feel so lonely when he disappeared into dreamland and I worried about the shadowy branches outside our bedroom window. I also worried about the closet, and what might be happening inside it while we slept. I was afraid the spiders were building colonies in there.

THE SOUNDS

The poem is full of "s's" and "c's" – the two initial letters in the title. That might be just a coincidence, but "s" is also the first letter of "sleep" and many "s's" recurring in a poem create the hissing tide of sleep washing up on two kids in bed who don't really want to go to sleep yet. Sounds repeating inside a poem create their own texture.

THE SLIGHTLY MYSTERIOUS ENDING

I'm completely intrigued by how two people who grow up in the same family can turn out to be entirely different. My brother and I, as adults, have very little in common. Our attitudes and ideas on most things – politics, hobbies, pleasures,

60

travels — are perfectly opposite. We are probably
as different as two people could be. He eats only
meat, I eat only vegetables. He lives in a huge new
house, I live in a tiny old cottage. We have
trouble communicating in words now. We get mad or
irritated easily, though "communication" is a
central part of both our jobs.

So I will always miss the brief period of time
when we felt close to one another and shared a room
and two ends of the same cord, and wanted to be
connected, even though it would feel much harder
later on. Falling asleep at different times was
just the beginning of a lifetime of differences.

I think poems always help us to look at what we
are connected to, and disconnected from. I could
not live without them.

A GHOULISH PROPOSAL

Two ghouls were dancing cheek to cheek
And each admired the other;
The ghoulie boy said, "Ghoulie girl,
You look just like my mother –
Your bloodshot gaze, your filthy ways,
Your grimy, hairy knees.
My ghoulie girl, my ugly one,
Oh will you marry me?"

The ghoulie girl was overcome
At what her partner said;
She blushed a bashful purple
And she punched him in the head.
"You smell of cheese, you're full of fleas,
You're really on the nose…
Oh ghoulie boy, my stinky one,
Let's do as you propose!"

The wedding was at twelve o'clock
The night of Hallowe'en;
The dark was filled with mournful howls
And agonizing screams.
The ghastly two have vowed anew
To fight both loud and often,
And they have put down payment on
A mouldy double coffin.

SALLY FARRELL ODGERS

A GHOULISH PROPOSAL: COMMENTARY

When I was young, in the 1960s, most poetry for
children was "nice" and "pretty", or else it was
the kind of poem you studied at school, which meant
it had probably been written 50 or more years ago.
I didn't like the first kind of poetry, but I did
like some of the second.

In fact, I have loved poetry all my life, and
I started writing it for fun while I was still in
primary school. I always wanted it to rhyme and
scan, but for no word to be used just because it
rhymed. I used to write about flowers, trees and
animals. Unlike most of my contemporaries, I never
wrote free verse or miserable poems about how badly
misunderstood I was. A little later in the 1970s, I
began writing fantasy poetry, and that is the kind
I mostly write these days.

Because I find writing in rhyme very easy, and
because I have a fairly large vocabulary (mostly
from reading so much poetry and so many books when
I was younger), I wrote a rhyming picture book in
1983. The publisher began putting out anthologies
of poetry for children and asked me to contribute.
I soon found that they didn't want my nature or
fantasy poetry. What they were after was cheeky,
funny and rather shocking poems. So I wrote quite a
few and had quite a few accepted. It was during
this period that I wrote "A Ghoulish Proposal".

If you look at "A Ghoulish Proposal", you will
see how it blends what the publishers asked for
with what I prefer to write. It is fantasy. It
rhymes. It scans. It has words that are specific,
and which say exactly what I wanted them to say. It
is also funny, cheeky and a little bit shocking.
Its humour comes from the fact that this is a love

story between two characters whose ideas and
expectations are not what one would usually find. I
had to use a kind of illogical logic to get the
tone right.

What is illogical logic? Well, if I was writing
a poem called "Delicious Smells" from a dog's point
of view, it would be all about smells dogs love,
like meat and yucky things, even though I like the
smell of flowers and fruit. For "A Ghoulish
Proposal", I looked at falling in love from a
ghoul's point of view. Since the ghouls have rather
horrible habits, I used illogical logic to find out
what they would find attractive in a boyfriend or
girlfriend. The ghoulie boy, for example, says
things to his girl which human girls would find
insulting. She loves it! And to show how much she
loves him, she punches him in the head and insults
him right back. Of course, they decide to get
married at Hallowe'en. Instead of singing and
wishing them luck, the characters that come to the
wedding scream and howl.

Once I had decided on the angle and used my
illogical logic, it was just a matter of plotting
the poem and finding the rhymes. "Other" and
"mother" rhyme, for example;"Knees" and "me" are
not an exact rhyme, but they are close enough.
I have always preferred rhymes that are close, and
which say exactly what I want, to rhymes that are
exact and might sound forced.

In line 5, in each of the three verses, I used
internal rhyme. "Gaze, ways", "cheese, fleas",
"two, anew" are all perfect rhyme. Other quite
interesting things about this poem are the use of
dialogue and some consonance and alliteration.
Consonance is not the same as rhyme, but it does
give a similar effect. For example, the third line
in the third verse says, "The dark was filled with

64

mournful howls." The words "filled", "mournful", and "howls" all have a strong "l"-sound in them. If you look at the first line in that third verse, you see the wedding was at twelve o'clock. This line has two strong "w"-sounds, and there is another one in the next line in the word "Hallowe'en". In the second last line, "and they have put down payment on" has strong "p"-sounds and "t"-sounds.

You can find this kind of wordplay throughout the poem. If you look at the first verse again, you will see a selection of words that all have a strong consonance. These include, "ghoulie", "filthy", "grimy", "hairy", "ugly", and "marry". The second verse uses alliteration including "ghoulie girl", "blushed a bashful", "full of fleas". The poem also relies on familiar phrases. Lines such as "dancing cheek to cheek", "will you marry me", "put a downpayment on" — things you are quite likely to have heard before. It's all part of the illogical logic.

It is rather strange looking back on this poem after almost 20 years. I have learned a great deal about writing since that time, and now I recognize quite a few of the tricks I used then. The funny thing is that I don't think I did a lot of it deliberately. I certainly thought up the rhymes on purpose, but I'm fairly sure the consonance and some of the alliteration was accidental. Or, maybe "accidental" is not quite what I mean. Perhaps I mean "instinctive", or "subconscious".

"A Ghoulish Proposal" is a long way in content from the beautiful older poetry of Herrick, Tennyson and Frost, but it uses some of the same kinds of wordplay. It seems that somewhere in the back of my mind is the idea that this is the way poetry is supposed to be.

THE KRAKEN

Deep beneath the foaming billows
something's suddenly amiss
as a creature wakes from slumber
in the bottomless abyss.
And a panic fills the ocean,
every fish in frenzy flees,
for the kraken has awakened
at the bottom of the seas.

It rises to the surface
with an overwhelming noise
and it hunts for mighty vessels
which it crushes and destroys.
Then it chokes a great leviathan
with one stupendous squeeze –
oh the kraken has awakened
at the bottom of the seas.

How it lashes, how it thrashes,
how it flashes, how it flails,
how it dwarfs the greatest fishes,
even dwarfs the mighty whales!
Nothing living in the ocean
can enjoy a moment's ease,
for the kraken has awakened
at the bottom of the seas.

JACK PRELUTSKY

THE KRAKEN: COMMENTARY

In the early 1970s, I was doing summer workshops
for children at a public library in Cambridge,
Massachusetts. I'd had about ten books of my poetry
for children published, and was thinking about what
to write next. All of my books until then had been
humorous, and I felt that I was getting into a rut.
I asked the children's librarian what sort of
poetry she thought her young readers would most
enjoy. She immediately came up with two topics –
monsters and dinosaurs. As soon as she said that,
I knew she was right. I decided to tackle monsters
first.

I thought back to my days as a not-so-well-
behaved little boy who generally declined to obey
his mother. For example, when I was about four or
five years old, my mother would notice that I ate
everything on my plate but the vegetables. "Eat
your vegetables," she'd say. "No!" I'd reply. Her
voice would get very soft, and she'd practically
whisper, "Eat your vegetables, or the bogeyman's
going to get you." Without further complaint,
I immediately ate all my vegetables.

When I began work on my monster book, which
eventually became "Nightmares", subtitled "Poems To
Trouble Your Sleep", the first poem I wrote was
"The Bogeyman", because that was the creature I
most remembered from my own childhood. Then I
continued with poems about other beings from
traditional, well-known folklore, such as vampires,
witches, wizards, ogres and trolls. The book was
beautifully illustrated with pen and ink drawings
by Arnold Lobel, and was an immediate success.
I called my editor and proposed doing a sequel.
She readily agreed, and I set to work.

This time I had to do a bit more research than I'd done for "Nightmares", since some of the creatures I intended to write about were relatively unfamiliar to me. These included the banshee, the poltergeist, the abominable snowman, and the kraken.

I read extensively on the kraken, and was fascinated by sailors' tales of this mammoth sea monster dragging ships to their doom. Sometimes the kraken was described as a giant octopus, sometimes as a monstrous whale, and occasionally as a colossal crab. In all cases, it was an undeniably fearsome creature.

I also loved the sound of the word kraken, and used it as an internal rhyme in the poem: hence, the kraken has awakened. When I recorded the book, "The Headless Horseman Rides Tonight", in which the poem appears, I emphasized the "kraken has awakened" rhyme. I learned years later that I'd made a fundamental error - I'd never verified the pronunciation of kraken. I'd assumed that the word rhymed with waken - after all, it certainly looked as if it did - but I was wrong. It's actually pronounced "CROCK-in". Recently I've checked every online dictionary, and to my chagrin, have found that kraken is always pronounced "CROCK-in", never "CRAY-kin".

If I had done my homework and checked its pronunciation when I wrote the poem over thirty years ago, I wouldn't have written "The Kraken" the way I did. I suspect that the poem I might have written wouldn't be as good as this one - of course, there's no telling. Anyhow, now you must read, "the CROCK-in has awakened". It's really not so bad, and I'm starting to get used to it.

EXCUSE ME, IS THIS INDIA?

I hopped into a three-wheeled car
And called out "Take me there!"
The driver started off at once,
He never asked me "Where?"

Suddenly he stopped and said,
"At last we're getting near."
"Near to what?" I asked him.
He bellowed in my ear:
"Near to this is far from that!
I think that's very clear!"

Though it wasn't clear to me,
I nodded very cleverly.

At a shop I stopped to see
If I could get a hint
Of where I was, but all I saw
Were clothes of every tint.

"Where am I and what's this place?"
I asked of everyone.
A woman came and said to me,
"You're as far as you can run.
But if you learn to fly, then you
Could catch up with the sun."

I left the shop
With a happy hop.

I hopped until the airport
And there! There was a sign.
But suddenly I realized
I couldn't read a line.

I asked a bearded gentleman.
He said, "Oh don't you know?
It doesn't matter where you are
But where you want to go."

I sat down there
And scratched my head,
And thought of what
The man had said.

ANUSHKA RAVISHANKAR

EXCUSE ME, IS THIS INDIA?: COMMENTARY

This excerpt is from a book called "Excuse Me, Is This India?" The illustrator, Anita Leutwiler, is a textile artist who lives in Germany. When she came to India, she collected bits and pieces of colourful cloth, and used them to make quilted pictures of things she had seen — cows on the beach, bandicoots in the garden and three-wheeled cars called autorickshaws.

I looked at the pictures, and wrote a story in verse about a child who turns into a blue mouse and sets off on a fantastic journey to a strange place, where the most unlikely things happen. When I started writing it, though, I wasn't very sure what it was going to be about. All I knew was that it was about a mouse who goes on a journey. Sometimes things just happen as you write, and it's difficult to explain how. That kind of writing is fun; it's like playing. You kick the words around, not getting too worked up about whether they're going in the right direction. Sometimes they don't, and you tear them up and start again. Sometimes they do, and to your surprise and delight you have a poem!

Usually, a book is written first, and then an illustrator creates pictures to go with the words. But this book happened the other way round. When you look carefully at a picture, lots of ideas start shooting off in different directions in your head. The difficult part is weaving all these images and ideas neatly into a story that you want to tell. And when you're writing the story in verse, there's another complication, which should not be taken lightly — the lines have to rhyme!

Trying to do this without sounding silly, killing grammar or changing spelling (which I often feel like doing) has turned many a writer bald. There have been times when I've gone through the alphabet – at, bat, brat, cat, chat, drat, doormat – right up to z, and not found a word that would fit. When that happens, you either decide to give up writing and take a job licking envelopes in the post office, or you cunningly change the previous line and end it with a word for which you can easily find a rhyme.

But there are also times when the right word floats into your head a moment before you write it, and who can tell where it came from? It happens rarely. Most of the time writing is a lot of sweating and hair-pulling and ink-splattering.

In the poem, the journey of the blue mouse has the unreal, random feel of a dream, where events need not make sense at all. The blue mouse goes from place to place asking the cow, the bandicoots, the elephant and the humans she meets the same question in different ways: "Where am I?" Each of them gives her an outrageous and completely nonsensical answer, which baffles her even more.

The verse in this book is mostly nonsense verse, which is a special kind of verse. It seems to make sense, but if you read it carefully, you realize it's quite absurd, and means nothing. For example, the woman in the shop tells the blue mouse: "But if you learn to fly, then you/Could catch up with the sun."

The blue mouse is perfectly satisfied with this answer and leaves the shop with a happy hop. But in fact those lines are nonsensical, as is most of this poem. It may not teach you much about India, but it might leave you hopping happily.

SKIP DON'T TRIP

Skip don't trip
the rope's a whip

goes round and round
dabs the ground

a regular beat
for lively feet

to cross with a quick
shuffle a flick

or whisk of the heel
at times you feel

the rope miss
by a whisper a kiss

but don't stop now
it won't allow

the least lapse
suddenly slaps

the ground to make
quite sure you're awake

will dance to its tune
all afternoon

its whip whoop
its swish and swoop

its whizz and clip
its skip skip skip

CHRISTOPHER REID

SKIP DON'T TRIP: COMMENTARY

"Skip Don't Trip" is from "All Sorts", my first
book for children. Many of the poems in it are
about children, too. This one is placed next to
a sort of sonnet that describes a pair of boys
sharing a skateboard: one has a leg in plaster and
is pushing the board along with his crutch, while
his friend stands behind as a passenger. I saw this
sight one day, near where I live, and because I
admired both the cleverness and the daring of it –
and they were managing it very gracefully – I
wanted to put it into verse. "Skip Don't Trip" is
about another, more frequently seen playground
activity: skipping.

Because skipping is so common, we tend to take
it for granted, scarcely bothering to stop and look
if we don't happen to be actively involved. But it
is an amazing thing, difficult to do and exciting
to watch when it is done with flair. Many of the
different rhymes and chants that go with it are
worth listening to as well.

I suppose when I began my poem, what I should
most have liked was to produce an actual skipping
rhyme, for use in the playground, but that would
have been less easy – impossible, really. The point
about such rhymes is that children themselves have
made them up. They belong to children alone and,
unlike poems in books, have not been supplied by
adults or given the questionable blessing of adult
approval. They are often as lively as they are just
because they are rough and rude, and this makes
them both fun to chant and a stimulating
accompaniment to the serious business of not
letting your feet get tangled in a fast-moving rope
that will show no mercy if you put a foot wrong.

Although I knew I couldn't write a proper
skipping rhyme, I soon saw that I could write
something like it: a poem that might encourage the
reader's mind to skip acrobatically. The most
obvious oddity of "Skip Don't Trip" is its lack of
punctuation. Punctuation marks make pauses — but
a skipping-rope won't stop for even the shortest
rest, so punctuation had to go, leaving the reader
to pick up the beat by ear alone. The rhymes and
line-breaks are there to help, and by reading the
poem several times it should be possible to catch
the beat and reach the end without getting in a
tangle. In actual skipping, the rhythm of the rope
and the movement of the feet must be timed slightly
differently — what musicians call "syncopation".
Making this work needs practice, whether in jazz,
in skipping, or in a poem like this one, which may
look difficult at first sight, but can be managed
if you keep at it. The reward should be the
pleasure of feeling your mind dance a little more
nimbly than you thought it was able to.

THIRTY-TWO LAPS

One Tuesday when I was about
Ten
I swam thirty-two laps
Which is one mile.
And when I climbed out of the water
I felt like a big, fat lump of jelly
And my legs were like rubber
And there was this huge man
There
With tremendous muscles all
Over him
And I went up to him and said
"I've just swum a mile."
And he said,
"How many laps was that then?"
"Thirty-two," I said.
And the man said,
"I've got a lad here who can do ninety."

MICHAEL ROSEN

THIRTY-TWO LAPS: COMMENTARY

"Thirty-Two Laps"is the true story of what happened
when I swam a mile at what used to be called Harrow
Swimming Baths, not far from Harrow-on-the-Hill
underground station. I used to spend a lot of time
at this pool when I was around ten years old but
I didn't belong to their swimming club. I've
sometimes found that people who run sports clubs at
places where the public can go get quite irritated
if a kid from outside the sports club does as well
as one of their kids. I guess that that's what was
going on here.

This extra fact has got absolutely nothing
whatsoever to do with the poem but you heard it
here first: I was born just round the corner from
the baths.

Sometimes people ask me why I write poems that
don't rhyme, that seem to sound like short
paragraphs, or even short speeches.

The answer is that when I was young, the poems
I liked were quite often ones that didn't rhyme,
that sounded like speech, or like a stream of
thought. One writer who wrote like this was Dylan
Thomas in his play "Under Milk Wood", and another
was the American poet, Carl Sandburg, who wrote
poems that sounded like someone talking onto the
page.

So when I started writing, that was the sound
that I tried to imitate. As I got older I found out
that many poets had written like this, for over a
hundred years - particularly in France, Germany and
America.

If I ask myself what I'm trying to achieve, all
I can say is that I find this way of writing helps
me get to what I think is the real truth of a

moment or a scene from my life. I can explore it for what really happened and how I feel about what happened by trying to capture what people were saying, what I could see and what I could hear.

People have sometimes said to me that this is an unusual way of writing for children. Well, if it's unusual, then I say three cheers for that.

If you want to sell millions of books, the best thing to do is to write in a way that's "usual", or very familiar. I always think that the best way to write for anyone, children included, is to write in ways that are UNfamiliar, in ways that make people surprised or curious. One of the jobs of a writer is to make familiar things unfamiliar and to make unfamiliar things familiar. That's what I always try to do.

I realise that this annoys some people. It makes them very irritated, because they say that what I write "isn't poetry". Well, I just say, call it something else, then. Don't worry about what it's called. Call it "stuff" or "thingies" or "pieces" and put it on one side, rather as the zoologists had to do when they first saw the duck-billed platypus.

Actually, come to think of it, why not call what I write "duck-billed platypus"?

BELLICOSE BRIGAND
vs BELLIGERENT BEAR

A bear and a brigand were bickering bitterly
Under the shade of a baobab tree.
"The best thing by far," bawled the brigand, "is baklava."
"Bosh!" boomed the bear. "It can't possibly be."

"Why, there's bric-a-brac, ipecac, blubber, and broccoli,
Bamboo, banana oil, beetles, and brine."
"You bandy-legged brute," brayed the brigand, "you
blatherskite!
Baklava beats them all any old time."

Oh what a brouhaha: "Baklava! Balderdash!
Bah!" barked the bear. "We shall never agree."
"Let us pause," breathed the brigand, "and banish this
blabber with hot buttered bat bread and barnacle tea."

JEANNE STEIG

BELLICOSE BRIGAND vs
BELLIGERENT BEAR: COMMENTARY

The question is, Why do I write?
Ah, well, the page, you see, is white,

And I've a thing or two to say.
They're dumb? I'll write them anyway.

I write because I love each word,
I love them more when they're absurd.

The cock-a-mamey ones that jig,
The ones that zag, the ones that zig:

Like flim-flam, hanky-panky, and
Mish-mash or nit-wit — both are grand.

Some words are soft and sneaky, too:
Lumbago, kibosh, ooze, kazoo.

Rambunctious words are pure delight,
There's yuk-a-puck, there's fly-by-night,

They rattle in my head until
I turn them loose. They're rather shrill.

Why do I write? I write because
there is a hunger there that gnaws.

It's like a sort of crazy itch
That stretches to a fever-pitch,

I need to scratch — what else will do?
Not dollar bills, not cheese fondue,

Not fancy boots, not love, not crime:
I've got to sit me down and rhyme.

There is the subject. That will come.
And rhythm, like an echoing drum,

And there are rules one has to keep,
The way musicians bloop and bleep

While keeping time, so they can play
In any hog-wild, tomfool way,

And no ill-wisher dares to state
It makes his blood coagulate

To hear such ring-tailed, roistering notes,
The bleating of a gang of goats.

I'll bet you figured I'd forgot
The reader. No, no, I have not.

For what's the good of writing if
It can't be shared? T'would bore me stiff.

I do love words. And, as I've said,
I write in order to be read.

COWS ON THE BEACH

Two cows,
fed-up with grass, field, farmer,
barged through barbed wire
and found the beach.
Each mooed to each:
This is a better place to be,
a stretch of sand next to the sea,
this is the place for me.
And they stayed there all day,
strayed this way, that way,
over to rocks,
past discarded socks,
ignoring the few people they met
(it wasn't high season yet).
They dipped hooves in the sea,
got wet up to the knee,
they swallowed pebbles and sand,
found them a bit bland,
washed them down with sea-water,
decided they really ought to
rest for an hour.

Both were sure
they'd never leave here.
Imagine, they'd lived so near
and never knew!
With a swapped moo
they sank into sleep,
woke to the yellow jeep
of the farmer
revving there,
feet from the incoming sea.
This is no place for cows to be,
he shouted, and slapped them
with seaweed, all the way home.

MATTHEW SWEENEY

COWS ON THE BEACH:
COMMENTARY

What I remember about the writing of "Cows on the Beach" is this: I was back in Donegal, where I come from, staying in a house close to the sea. One day I decided to take a walk down there. There were no people on the beach, but right at the water's edge two cows were stepping through the little waves. I was so surprised by this that I ran back to the house to get the camera – at that time *The Observer* newspaper was offering £100 for an unusual photograph, and I was sure the next £100 would be mine. When I got there I realised that my wife had gone off in the car and taken the camera with her, so I had to make do with putting the cows in a poem instead.

I started by asking questions, as I usually do when beginning a poem. How often had they visited the beach? Did they like it there? What did the farmer think of them being there? Very quickly I decided the poem had to be from the cows' perspective, even though I wanted to keep it in the third person – and there had to be a bit of cow-speak in it (whenever I read the poem aloud to young children, I say those lines in a mooey way). I felt this was one poem that had to rhyme, but there had to be a flexibility about the lineation – sometimes long lines, sometimes short. And the farmer had to speak (or shout) at the end, to balance the cows speaking earlier. But all this makes it sound like I worked out the poem like a piece of maths. In reality, like the best poems often do, it wrote itself – or more properly, it set its own course and all I had to do was steer.

MATERIALS

Growing up, I
did not have books

The only reading material
there was

were old newspapers laid out
on the floor

to dry
our winter boots

or wrap
things of glass

When I learned to read,
the winter boots

lay dripping
in the hallway,

the glass, broken
and uncovered

because I knew this
this

would be my way in.

SOUVANKHAM THAMMAVONGSA

MATERIALS: COMMENTARY

I used to make my own books and take them to small
press and zine fairs and people often asked me what
they were about. I got tired of explaining what
I was doing and why it was important. So I wrote an
introduction to my handmade books. When I put
together the manuscript of my first published book,
I turned this explanation into a poem. I thought
about all the people who might one day read it in
libraries, in bookstores, in their homes. I wanted to
tell them why I was there, but, more than anything,
I wanted to say that if they wanted to be a writer
too it was possible. That I, who had come from a home
without books and a language that wasn't mine, had
used the experience to reach people like me.

It is something I wish someone had said to me
when I was a child.

My parents bought newspapers to put under our
winter boots to dry them. The newspaper absorbed
water better than a carpet and soaked newspapers
dried faster. The newspaper was also used to wrap
glass things so they wouldn't break.

How I use and think of language is a lot like
how my parents used that newspaper. It's a matter
of being resourceful, of using what is there and
making it work and matter in different ways.

I set up the poem so that all the materials
appear in the first few lines and reappear again
but hold a different meaning as I close the poem.

There is nothing complicated in what I did.
I just wanted to speak honestly to people whose
language isn't English and to show them it's
possible to use a language that isn't yours and
make it your own.

THE DISAPPEARING ALPHABET

Without the letter I, there'd be
No word for your IDENTITY,
And so you'd find it very tough
To tell yourself from other stuff.
Sometimes, perhaps, you'd think yourself
A jam jar on the pantry shelf.
Sometimes, perhaps, you'd make a
ticking sound
And slowly move your hands around.
Sometimes you'd lie down like a rug,
Expecting to be vacuumed. Ugh!
Surely my friends, you now see why
We need to keep the letter I.

RICHARD WILBUR

THE DISAPPEARING ALPHABET:
COMMENTARY

Children are often logical and literate; certainly
mine were, and when they were growing up I
delighted with them in the logic and illogic of
Lear and Carroll, and in all sorts of games with
words. When I took to writing my several books for
children, I wrote out of that family experience and
a home-grown sense of what might amuse a child.
With my children in mind, I did two little books of
poems and drawings, one called "Opposites" and the
other called "More Opposites".

Sometimes, as in this example, the "Opposites"
poems were plausible as to what's opposed to what:
"What is the opposite of riot?/It's lots of people
keeping quiet."

At other times, the attempt to force the world
into neat antitheses was arbitrary and absurd. The
poems appealed, I think, both to the children's
desire for order and to their taste for a measure
of honest chaos.

Another book of mine, "The Pig in the Spigot",
consisted of little poems which strove to explain,
in some far-fetched manner, why - for instance - we
find the word "hick" inside the word "chicken".

It's seldom that you see a hen or cock
Come strolling down a busy city block.
They much prefer the country for their part,
Because a *chicken* is a *hick* at heart.

And here is another small specimen from that book:

Moms weep when children don't do as they say.
That's why there is a *sob* in *disobey*.

When I began to write poems for a sequel to that
book, I found myself publishing groups of them in
grown-up magazines like the "Atlantic Monthly",
under the title "Words Inside of Words: for
Children and Others". All of my children's books
have, in fact, sought to be the sort of thing which
can be enjoyed by adults and children, together or
apart. It made me happy to learn, a few years ago,
that a woman whom I esteemed kept a copy of
"Opposites" in her bathroom.

"The Disappearing Alphabet" is based on the
notion that words are our key to reality and that
the loss of any letter would cause some part of
reality to escape us. Looking now at my lines about
the letter "I", I can imagine a nightmarish
children's book editor who would say that
"identity" is too hard a word for young children.
I have never met such an editor, but I believe they
exist, depriving children of variety and challenge.

BLAKE LEADS A WALK ON THE MILKY WAY

He gave silver shoes to the rabbit
and golden gloves to the cat
and emerald boots to the tiger and me
and boots of iron to the rat.

He inquired, "Is everyone ready?
The night is uncommonly cold,
We'll start on our journey as children,
but I fear we will finish it old."

He hurried us to the horizon
where morning and evening meet.
The slippery stars went skipping
under our hapless feet.

"I'm terribly cold," said the rabbit.
"My paws are becoming quite blue,
and what will become of my right thumb
while you admire the view?"

"The stars," said the cat, "are abundant
and falling on every side.
Let them carry us back to our comforts.
Let us take the stars for a ride."

"I shall garland my room," said the tiger,
"with a few of these emerald lights."
"I shall give up sleeping forever," I said.
"I shall never part day from night."

The rat was sullen. He grumbled
he ought to have stayed in his bed.
"What's gathered by fools in heaven
will never endure," he said.

Blake gave silver stars to the rabbit
and golden stars to the cat
and emerald stars to the tiger and me
but a handful of dirt to the rat.

NANCY WILLARD

BLAKE LEADS A WALK ON THE MILKY WAY: COMMENTARY

CONVERSATION BETWEEN THE POEM AND ITS AUTHOR

The Poem: Dear author, though we know each other very well, there are a few questions I have always wanted to ask you.

The Author: Ask away. I also have a few questions I've always wanted to ask you.

The Poem: Fair enough. What gave you the idea of writing me?

The Author: Now that's a good question. Before I answer let me remind you that you are only one of sixteen poems in a book called A VISIT TO WILLIAM BLAKE'S INN. The poems in that book will show you what it's like to spend a few days at an inn run by the poet William Blake. You arrive, you meet new friends. Mr Blake enjoys taking his guests out on walks through the neighbourhood, and one of his favourite walks is the Milky Way.

It also happens to be one of mine, though of course I can only walk it in my imagination, and that's one reason I wrote the poem. In the poem I describe the sky as chilly and bright with stars. That is how the sky always looks to me on a clear night. There are two kinds of guests who take this walk: those who love to go star-gathering (rather like gathering sea shells) and those who complain about the cold. To help you see and hear the characters taking this walk, I let them speak for themselves. I have always loved dialogue, both in stories and poems.

The Poem: Blake gave such lovely gifts to the rabbit and the cat and the tiger—

The Author: Ah yes, silver shoes and silver

stars, golden gloves and golden stars, and emerald
boots and emerald stars.

The Poem: But to the rat he gave boots of iron —

The Author: Boots of iron are very practical. So
is the rat. He's a bit grumpy, isn't he? He would
rather be comfortably curled up in bed than go out
exploring on the Milky Way. And for this reason the
stars do not look beautiful to him at all. It's the
light in ourselves that helps us to see beauty in
others. And now, my dear poem, I want to ask you a
question.

The Poem: Ask away.

The Author: Why did you want to rhyme? When you
popped into my head, I heard the music in you
before I even knew the words. It's just as if you
were on the other side of the water —

The Poem: What water?

The Author: When you are rowing on a lake, you
can hear voices from a great way off. You can't see
who is speaking but you can almost hear what they
are saying. That's what you sounded like before I
could hear the words.

The Poem: You have answered your own question. I
could say that I arrived in rhyme because it is
easier to remember poems that rhyme than those that
don't and I do want to be remembered. But that's
not the whole story. Mr Blake wrote poems that
rhymed, and since I'm bringing news of William
Blake's Inn, I want to convey it in a way that
might have pleased him.

The Author: You know, when I wrote those rhymed
lines, I tried to write in a language that is no
different from the language we speak every day.
I wanted both the words and the order of the words
to sound natural, as if speaking in rhyme were the
most natural thing in the world. Of course that
didn't happen in the first draft. You, my dear

95

poem, went through numerous revisions. It took
a lot of revisions to make you sound as if I hadn't
laboured over you at all.

The Poem: Would you have written me differently
if I had not been one of sixteen poems about the
inn?

The Author: Probably not. But I think that
writing several poems about characters that all
live in one place makes the writing process easier.
You don't have to pack all your characters and
images into a single poem. The tiger and the cat
and the rabbit appear in their own poems elsewhere.
My purpose in writing you was simple: I wanted to
tell a story. And I have you to thank, my dear
poem, for helping me do it.

biographical notes

JOHN AGARD is a playwright, poet, and children's writer from Guyana, who came to England in 1977. He worked for the Commonwealth Institute from 1978 to 1985, travelling all over the UK as a touring reader, promoting Caribbean culture in schools. He was the first Writer in Residence at the South Bank Centre in London and Poet in Residence at the BBC. He has won five awards for his work, including the Paul Hamlyn Award for Poetry in 1997 and a Cholmondeley Award in 2004. His latest collection, 'We Brits', was shortlisted for the 2007 British Book Awards Decibel Writer of the Year award. John Agard lives in Lewes, near Brighton, with his partner, the poet Grace Nichols.

www.contemporarywriters.com

PHILIP DE VOS was a language teacher and afterwards an opera singer and photographer. In 1998 he made a CD in which he sang musical arrangements of his poems. Known in South Africa as a writer of nonsense verse and stories, he has published 25 books in Afrikaans as well as a book of his photographs and has been awarded several literary prizes for his work. He also published two volumes of verses in English: 'Carnival of the Animals' and 'Beware of the Canary!' He specialises in rhyming translations, for which he has received two international IBBY awards. He lives in Cape Town.

www.stellenboschwriters.com

CAROL ANN DUFFY was born in Glasgow and grew up in England. Her anthology, 'Stopping for Death', won the 2007 Signal Poetry Award. She writes for both children and adults. She received an Eric Gregory Award in 1984, a Cholmondeley Award in 1992, the Dylan Thomas Award from the Poetry Society in 1989 and a Lannan Literary Award from the Lannan Foundation in 1995. Her latest collection of poetry, 'Rapture', won the T.S. Eliot Award. Carol Ann Duffy lives in Manchester and is Creative Director of the Writing School at Manchester Metropolitan University.

www.contemporarywriters.com

JACKIE KAY was born and brought up in Scotland. Her most recent collection of short stories, 'Wish I Was Here', was published in 2007 to great acclaim. She has won the Guardian Fiction Prize for her novel, 'Trumpet', and a Forward

Prize for her collection of poetry, 'The Adoption Papers'. Jackie Kay lives in Manchester with her son and teaches literature at the University of Newcastle. www.contemporarywriters.com

X. J. KENNEDY was born in 1929 in Dover, New Jersey, and at the age of fourteen published a magazine called 'Terrifying Test-tube Tales'. He attended various universities – Seton Hall, Columbia, the Sorbonne, Michigan – served in the U.S. Navy and taught at various colleges. His collections of poems for adults include 'In a Prominent Bar in Secaucus: New & Selected Poems and Peeping Tom's Cabin: Comic Verse'. His children's books include collections of verse and two novels, and he has written several textbooks, among them 'An Introduction to Poetry' with Dana Gioia, now in its eleventh edition. X. J. Kennedy and his wife, author Dorothy M. Kennedy, live in Lexington, Massachusetts, where they earn their bread as freelance writers and sometimes read aloud to six grandchildren. www.XJandDorothyMKennedy.com

JONARNO LAWSON was born in Hamilton, Canada. His second book of poetry for children, 'Black Stars in a White Night Sky', received the 2007 Lion and Unicorn Award for Excellence in North American Poetry. 'The Man in the Moon-Fixer's Mask' was an honour book for the same award in 2005. 'A Voweller's Bestiary', a book of animal lipograms for children, will be published in 2008. He is also the author of two books of poetry and aphorisms for adults, 'Love is an Observant Traveller' and 'Inklings'. JonArno Lawson lives in Toronto with his wife and two children. ca.geocities.com/jonarno@rogers.com

DENNIS LEE was born in Toronto, Canada, where he was recently the city's first Poet Laureate. He has written more than twenty books for adults and children, as well as the song lyrics for Jim Henson's television series, 'Fraggle Rock'. His books include 'Alligator Pie', 'Garbage Delight', 'Jelly Belly', 'Bubblegum Delicious' and 'So Cool'. Dennis Lee lives in Toronto and has three children and two grandsons. www.library.utoronto.ca/canpoetry/lee/

MARGARET MAHY is a well-known New Zealand author of children's and young adult books. Her books, 'The Haunting' and 'The Change Over', received the Carnegie Medal. She has written nearly 50 novels, including 'Alchemy' in 2002. Among her children's books, 'A Lion in the Meadow' and 'The Man Whose Mother was a Pirate' are considered national classics. Her novels have been translated into many different languages. In 2006 she was awarded the Hans Christian Andersen Award (known as the Little Nobel Prize) in recognition of a "lasting contribution to children's literature". Margaret Mahy lives on Banks Peninsula, Canterbury, in the South Island of New Zealand. library.christchurch.org.nz/MargaretMahy

ROGER McGOUGH was born in Liverpool, and is the author of over fifty books of poetry for adults and children and the editor of numerous anthologies. The winner of two BAFTAs and a Royal Television Society award, he also co-wrote the script for the 'Yellow Submarine' animation film. A Fellow of the Royal Society of Literature, he has a Cholmondeley Award and is a two-time winner of both the Signal and CLPE

Awards for the best book of poetry for children. He is an Honorary Professor of Thames Valley University and a Fellow of John Moores University, Liverpool. He was made a Freeman of the City of Liverpool in 2001 and received a CBE from the Queen in 2004 for services to literature. Currently he presents Poetry Please on BBC Radio 4. He lives in Barnes, south-west London with his wife and two of his four children.
www.rogermcgough.org.uk/

ADRIAN MITCHELL was born near Hampstead Heath, in London, in 1932. He writes poems, stories, plays and songs for adults and children. Mitchell's poems for children appear in 'Daft as a Doughnut' and 'Balloon Lagoon', both illustrated by Tony Ross. He lives with his wife, Celia, and their golden retriever, Daisy the Dog of Peace, near Hampstead Heath.
www.rippingyarns.co.uk/adrian/

STEPHEN MITCHELL'S many books include the bestselling 'Tao Te Ching', 'Bhagavad Gita', 'Meetings with the Archangel', 'Gilgamesh', and the forthcoming 'The Second Book of the Tao'. His books for young readers include 'The Wishing Bone', winner of the 2004 Lee Bennett Hopkins Poetry Award, 'Jesus: What He Really Said and Did' and 'Genies, Meanies, and Magic Rings'. He lives in California, in the United States.
www.stephenmitchellbooks.com

PAT MORA enjoys writing for both children and adults. She founded the family literacy initiative, El Día de los Niños/ El Día de los Libros, (Children's Day/ Book Day). and received an Honorary Doctorate in Letters from Buffalo State College (SUNY) in 2006. A speaker at conferences,

universities and schools, she won the 2006 National Hispanic Cultural Center Literary Award. She was also a Visiting Carruthers Chair at the University of New Mexico, a recipient and judge of the Poetry Fellowships from the National Endowment for the Arts and a recipient and advisor of the Kellogg National Leadership Fellowships. A former consultant, museum director, university administrator and teacher, Pat Mora is the mother of three adult children. She enjoys family/friend time, reading, gardening, cooking, museums and the wonder of the natural world when she travels and when she returns to her home in beautiful Santa Fe, New Mexico.
www.patmora.com

GRACE NICHOLS was born in Georgetown, Guyana, in 1950. After working in Guyana as a teacher and journalist, she emigrated to the UK in 1977. Her first collection of poetry, 'I Is a Long Memoried Woman' won the 1983 Commonwealth Poetry Prize. She has written several further books of poetry and a novel for adults, 'Whole of a Morning Sky'. Her books for children include collections of short stories and poetry anthologies. Her latest work, of new and selected poems, is 'Everybody Got a Gift'. She now lives in Lewes, near Brighton, with her partner, the poet John Agard.
www.contemporarywriters.com/

NAOMI SHIHAB NYE has written or edited more than 25 books, many for young readers, including 'This Same Sky' and 'The Space Between Our Footsteps'. She lives in San Antonio, Texas.
www.barclayagency.com/nye.hml

SALLY FARRELL ODGERS has been writing poetry for most of her life. In addition to her many poems in anthologies, she has produced rhyming picture books, the first of which, 'Dreadful David', has been in print for twenty-one years. She lives in Tasmania. www.sallyodgers.com/

JACK PRELUTSKY was born in Brooklyn, New York and is the author of more than fifty poetry collections. For over thirty years, he has been America's most popular children's poet. His award-winning books include 'The New Kid on the Block', 'The Dragons are Singing Tonight' and 'If Not for the Cat'. In 2006, the Poetry Foundation named Prelutsky the inaugural winner of the Children's Poet Laureate award. Jack Prelutsky lives in Seattle, Washington.
www.jackprelutsky.com

ANUSHKA RAVISHANKAR has written over 15 books of verse, fiction and non-fiction, many of which have been published internationally. The majority of these are nonsense or absurd verse, a genre she is particularly fond of. Several of her books have won international awards — 'Tiger on a Tree' was given the Star of Excellence by the National Union of Culture and Libraries in France in 1999, and 'Anything But a Grabooberry', 'Trash!', 'On Ragpicker Children' and 'Recycling' received prestigious special mentions in the International White Raven's Catalogue of the World's Best Children's Books in 2000 and 2001 respectively. Apart from children's books, she also writes plays for both children and adults. Anushka Ravishankar lives in Delhi, India with her family.
www.tarabooks.com/aboutus_authors.asp

CHRISTOPHER REID is a British poet, anthologist, publisher and teacher. He has been nominated twice for the Whitbread Awards: in 1996 and 2002. His books of poetry include 'Arcadia', which won the 1980 Somerset Maugham Award and the Hawthornden Prize; 'Pea Soup'; 'Katerina Brac'; 'In The Echoey Tunnel'; 'Expanded Universes'; 'For and After' and 'Mr Mouth'. He has also written two books of poems for children: 'All Sorts', which won the 2000 Signal Poetry Award, and 'Alphabicycle Order'. Most recently he edited the letters of Ted Hughes for Faber and Faber. Christopher Reid is now Professor in Creative Writing at the University of Hull.
www.contemporarywriters.com/

MICHAEL ROSEN is a children's novelist and poet and the author of 140 books including 'You Can't Catch Me', which won the Signal Poetry Award in 1982, 'We're Going on a Bear Hunt', winner of the Smarties Book Prize in 1990, 'The Sad Book', winner of the Smarties Prize in 2005 and 'Alphabet Poem', which won a WOW award in 2005. Michael Rosen was appointed the UK's fifth Children's Laureate in June 2007.
www.michaelrosen.co.uk/about.html

JEANNE STEIG is the author of several books of light verse and two books of prose, including 'Consider the Lemming', A Parents' Choice Remarkable Book in 1998, 'Alpha Beta Chowder', 'A Handful of Beans', a New York Times Book Review Best Illustrated Book in 1998, 'A Gift from Zeus: Sixteen Favorite Myths', a Publishers Weekly Best Book of the Year, Smithsonian Magazine's Notable

Book of the Year, and a New York Times Notable Book. They were all illustrated by her late husband, William Steig, with the exception of her newest release, 'Tales From Gizzard's Grill', which was illustrated by Sandy Turner. Her light verse has also been published in The New Yorker and in various literary magazines. Jeanne Steig lives in Boston, Massachusetts.

www.pippinproperties.com/authill/steigj/

MATTHEW SWEENEY'S publications for children include 'Up on the Roof: New and Selected Poems' and a novel, 'Fox'. He was a resident in Berlin in 2005-2006 as a guest of The German Academic Exchange Service DAAD, under their Invited Artists programme. His most recent book of poems is 'Black Moon' published by Cape. He is the co-author of 'Writing Poetry' and the editor of several anthologies. Matthew Sweeney lives in Berlin.

www.writersartists.net/msweeney.htm

SOUVANKHAM THAMMAVONGSA is the author of 'Small Arguments', which won the national ReLit Award in Canada in 2004. Her most recent book, 'Found', was published in 2007. Souvankham Thammavongsa lives in Toronto, Canada.
www.wier.ca/sthammavongsa.html

RICHARD WILBUR'S poems have won various awards, including two Pulitzers, and have recently been gathered in 'Collected Poems 1943-2004', which includes his children's verse as well. His translations of Molière and Racine are widely performed, and his latest effort in that vein is a rendering of Corneille's baroque masterpiece 'The Theatre of Illusion' ('L'Illusion Comique'). Richard

Wilbur lives in Cummington, Massachusetts.
www.english.uiuc.edu/maps/poets/s_z/wilbur/wilbur.htm

NANCY WILLARD is the author of two novels, twelve books of poetry and numerous books for children. She has edited one anthology of poems for young people, 'Step Lightly: Poems for the Journey'. 'A Visit to William Blake's Inn: Poems for Innocent and Experienced Travellers' was the first poetry book to win the Newbery Medal. Her most recent book, 'The Flying Bed' was published in 2007. She teaches in the English Department at Vassar College, New York State.

www.randomhouse.com/

acknowledgements

The editor and publisher gratefully acknowledge permission to use the following material:

Old World New World ©John Agard from Under the Moon and Over the Sea edited by John Agard and Grace Nichols, published by Walker Books, 2002, used with permission of Caroline Sheldon Literary Agency; Five Girls © Carol Ann Duffy from Meeting Midnight, published by Faber and Faber Ltd, 1999; Aquarium © Philip de Vos from Carnival of the Animals, published by Human and Rousseau, 1998; The Stincher © Jackie Kay from Three Has Gone, published by Blackie Children's Books, 1994, used with permission of PFD; Iguana © X. J. Kennedy from Did Adam Name the Vinegarroon?, published by David R. Godine, 1982 used with permission of Curtis Brown Ltd; The Octopus and the Seahorse © JonArno Lawson from The Man in the Moon-Fixer's Mask, published by Pedlar Press, 2004; Alligator Pie © Dennis Lee, published by Key Porter Books 1974; The Man from the Land of Fandango © Margaret Mahy from Nonstop Nonsense, published by Margaret K. McElderry Books, 1989, used with permission of Watson Little Ltd; Didgeridoo © Roger McGough from All the Best: The Selected Poems of Roger McGough, published by Puffin Books, 2004, used with permission of PFD; Riding West From Little Bear © Adrian Mitchell from Daft as a Doughnut, published by Orchard Books, 2004; The Wishing Bone © Stephen Mitchell, published by Candlewick Press, 2003; Colours Crackle, Colours Roar © Pat Mora from Confetti: Poems for Children, published by Lee and Low Books, 1996; Sun is Laughing © Grace Nichols from A Caribbean Dozen: Poems from Caribbean Poets edited by Grace Nichols and John Agard, published by Walker Books, 1994; Supple Cord © Naomi Shihab Nye from Amaze me: Poems for Girls, published by Greenwillow Books, 2005; A Ghoulish Proposal © Sally Farrell Odgers from Vile Verse, compiled by Jane Covernton, published by Omnibus, 1988 and unpublished manuscript Our Home is Dirt By Sea: Australian Children's Poets, Di Bates, 2005; The Kraken © Jack Prelutsky from The Headless Horseman Rides Tonight, published by Greenwillow Books, 1980; Excerpt from Excuse Me, Is This India? © Anushka Ravishankar, excerpted from the book Excuse Me, Is this India?, first published by Tara Publishing © 2001; Skip Don't Trip © Christopher Reid from All Sorts, published by Ondt and Gracehoper, 1999, used with permission of Ondt & Gracehoper; Thirty-Two Laps © Michael Rosen from Quick! Let's Get Out of Here, published by Andre Deutsch, 1983, used with permission of PFD; Bellicose Brigand vs Belligerent Bear © Jeanne Steig from Alpha Beta Chowder, published by HarperCollins Publishers, 1992, used with permission of Pippin Properties, Inc; Cows On The Beach © Matthew Sweeney from The Flying Spring Onion, published by Faber and Faber, 1992; Materials © Souvankham Thammavongsa from Small Arguments, published by Pedlar Press, 2003; excerpt from The Disappearing Alphabet © Richard Wilbur from The Disappearing Alphabet, published by Harcourt Children's Books, 2001; Blake Takes A Walk On The Milky Way © Nancy Willard from A Visit to William Blake's Inn: Poems for Innocent and Experienced Travellers, published by Harcourt Children's Books, 1981.

I would like to thank: Caroline Royds, my editor at Walker Books, whose idea this was, who made many helpful suggestions, and who made the whole experience a great deal of fun, and her hard-working and helpful assistant, Genevieve Herr;

My wife Amy, and my children, Sophie and Asher, for their support and always helpful input.

Lissa Paul who, through her books and conversation, introduced me to the work of many of the poets included here, and Michael Joseph for our essential and stimulating e-mail correspondence;

Dianne Bates, in whose unpublished manuscript of Australian children's poetry 'Our Home is Dirt by Sea', I discovered Sally Odger's poetry;

Bill Condon, Reviva Schermbrucker, Karabo Kgoleng, Richard Flynn, Joseph T. Thomas Jr. (Thomas's book 'Poetry's Playground' should be read by anyone interested in children's poetry),

Bob Barton, Nancy Chambers, Anne Harvey, June Factor, Celia Jellett, Maureen Nimon, Sara Fanelli, Lena Coakley at CANSCAIP, Peter Carver,

R.P. MacKintyre, John Foster, and Ms. Glendy Lee (Children's Librarian at the Hong Kong Public Library), for help with my research.

Finally, thank you to Claas Kazzer, whose website for the Signal Poetry Award also brought many fine poets and books to my attention.

JonArno Lawson